CLASSROOM CLOSE-UPS

A Guide to Using Video Technology in the Classroom

Bryan Berg

Good Apple

Executive Editor: Jeri Cipriano
Editor: Susan Eddy
Inside Illustration: Alex Bloch

GOOD APPLE
An Imprint of Modern Curriculum
A Division of Simon & Schuster
299 Jefferson Road, P.O. Box 480
Parsippany, NJ 07054-0480

ISBN: 1-56417-719-X 1 2 3 4 5 6 7 8 9 MAL 01 00 99 98 97 96

Table of Contents

Introduction 4

Scripting and Storyboarding 6

Language Arts and Literature

Hyperbole Theater 7

Literary Challenge 9

May I See Your Poetic License? 11

Two Minutes With 13

Video Newspaper 15

History and Social Studies

Cultural Perspectives 17

Distance Debate 20

Do You Want My Job? 22

Making Television History 24

Meet the Past 28

Video Travelogue 30

Science

Brighter Colors and Whiter Whites . .33

Mother Earth Would Be Proud 37

Tally Me Bananas 39

Voyage to the Bottom of the Sea . . .41

Winds of Change 44

Mathematics

Action Fractions 46

Math-a-Graph 48

Real World Math 50

The Math Shopping Network 52

Visual and Performing Arts

And Now, a Word from Our Sponsor .54

Critic's Corner 56

Karaoke™ TV 58

Telethon .60

Video-Surrealism 62

Miscellaneous

Public Service Announcement 64

See You in September 66

The Year in Review 67

Video Portfolio 69

Welcome to Our School 73

Reproducibles

Blank Script 75

Blank Storyboard 76

Pre-Taping Checklist 77

On-Line Computer Networks 78

Glossary .79

Introduction

As educators, we can't ignore the fact that today's children spend their formative years basking in the glow of electronic media. Nor can we continue to exclusively embrace teaching strategies that don't help students navigate the information superhighway. Given the technological strides of the past decade, we now have the opportunity to present curriculum in a manner that is both familiar and relevant to these children of the electronic era. As technology continues to be an integral part of students' lives, we can advocate technological literacy while promoting a thinking curriculum at the same time.

Video Technology in the Classroom

Using video technology as a teaching tool can be a step in the right direction. A TV, VCR, and camcorder have become commonplace at most schools. But the camcorder does not have to be relegated solely to recording and documenting school and classroom functions. In the hands of an inspired student, it is a magnificent instrument of creative expression and exploration.

Creative writing and the visual arts take on new dimensions when children write, perform, and videotape their own TV commercials. Science leaves the dry pages of texts and leaps into the real world through time-lapse photography of the oxidation process. Math proficiency becomes a prerequisite for students who produce a televised "Classroom Shopping" episode that challenges viewers to apply math skills as they calculate prices, discounts, and quantities.

Teaching the Lessons

Classroom Close-Ups offers a variety of lessons designed to provide teachers with plans for using video technology in the classroom. Many curricular areas are addressed in order to provide a range of educational alternatives from which to choose.

This medley of lessons will spark your imagination and inspire you to create interesting lessons that suit your needs. Feel free to modify the lessons offered to accommodate your style of teaching and the dynamics of your class. The more comfortable you are with the lessons, the more effective they will be.

Level of Experience

No prior video experience is necessary to use this book successfully. Just follow the step-by-step directions. Be patient with initial video productions—don't expect motion-picture quality. With each new project, however, competency increases, and it won't be long before your students become seasoned videographers.

Video Equipment Requirements

One VCR, one camcorder, and one TV are the only things you need to complete the lessons in this book. The projected time for each lesson assumes the availability of a single camcorder. However, the more camcorders that are available, the less time it will take to complete each lesson, as more than one production team will be able to shoot at the same time.

Cooperative Learning Groups

Most of the lessons require students to work in "production teams" or cooperative groups of four to six students. At the onset, be sure individual members understand the task at hand. Monitor each group's progress as it works and check to be sure that each member is actively engaged and the work load is fairly distributed.

Lesson Format

The lessons follow a traditional format, with behavioral objectives, materials, time and equipment requirements, and procedures. Lessons begin with brief descriptions to allow you to skim the book to locate activities pertinent to your needs. Finally, there are "helpful hints" designed to help you avoid the "glitches" of attempting any new procedure.

When to Use These Lessons

Start slowly. Choose a lesson you find interesting and try it. Be patient with early attempts and view mistakes as part of the learning process. You'll probably choose to work on one lesson at a time, spread out over the course of the year. Remember—the more time children spend with the equipment, the more proficient they will become.

With my own classes, I have teams of students tape assemblies, special events, and classroom activities for other teachers. My class produces a schoolwide morning broadcast that airs live in every classroom. My students show up every morning to turn on all the equipment and hook up all the cables. I let them run the show while I watch from the sidelines.

Ready On the Set

The next time you look at your students, think of them as writers, performers, artists, and technicians who are just waiting to begin their apprenticeships. You are in the privileged position of helping these students develop their craft while learning subject material that is vitally important to them.

Scripting and Storyboarding

The creation of a script and/or storyboard is an excellent and, in some cases, crucial organizational tool in video production. Scripts force students to create accurate "road maps" to specific destinations. They must decide where they are going and then plot how they will get there. Storyboards make students think visually and help them turn words into pictures. *A video must show, not tell.* Storyboards help make the transition.

A sample script can be found on page 19. A portion of a storyboard appears below. It need not document every detail of the video but should visually outline the content in an assortment of wide, medium, and close-up shots. Stick figures are perfectly adequate for a storyboard—it is nothing more than a visual outline.

Storyboard

Scene	Description	Picture	Time
6	Cut to video segment of travel agent seated at desk. Travel agent: *There is only one place on earth that will offer exactly what you want and more . . .*		:10
7	Cut to still image of French flag. Travel agent: *France!*		:10

Many of the activities in *Classroom Close-Ups* benefit from the creation of scripts and storyboards. For some, it is less important. Use scripts and storyboards as often as you feel it will benefit the students and their projects.

Reproducible worksheets for both are found on pages 75–76.

Hyperbole Theater

Students appear on videotape to add to an ongoing story that emphasizes exaggeration.

Objectives:

- To teach hyperbole as a tool in creative writing.
- To help students appreciate the power and beauty of language.
- To train students to write in a collaborative setting.

Video Equipment and Supplies:

- VCR
- camcorder
- television
- videotape
- paper
- pens or pencils

Time: 2–3 hours

Procedure:

1. Assign and discuss with students a story that uses exaggeration as a literary tool, such as a Paul Bunyon story. Define hyperbole as an intentional exaggeration not meant to be taken literally and invite students to cite examples from the story they have just read.

2. Divide students into small cooperative groups of 4 to 6 students. Explain that they will be writing a story featuring hyperbole. If you wish, you may write a few opening lines, such as the following, on the board.

Brandon was a strong man, although he really did not like to show it. He tended to be quiet and shy. But the events of that sleepy Sunday afternoon sent the entire town of Pleasantville into an uproar.

3.   Allow a few minutes for each group to write the next 2–3 lines of the story. Randomly select a group (roll dice or pull a number from a jar) and invite a member to read the group's lines.

4.   Select a student to videotape you reading the first two or three lines of the story, followed by a student reading the lines created by his or her group.

5.   Continue the process, adding selections from each group. It is important that all groups write continuously, even though not all their work will appear on the tape. Pause occasionally to discuss the direction of the story and to make suggestions, if necessary.

6.   Fifteen minutes before the period ends, encourage students to bring the story to a conclusion in the course of the next three or four contributions. The group producing the end of the tale may require some latitude in terms of time and number of lines. Record the last installment, rewind the tape, and play it for the class.

Helpful Hints

- Suggest to students that names of other students not be used in the story. Tell them you have the right to veto any lines you find crude or mean-spirited.

- Remind students that they will reap the benefits of legible writing or printing when they read before the camera. It's not a bad idea to have them read the lines once or twice to themselves before they are videotaped.

- Consider extending the activity by inviting students to illustrate portions of the story. You are then in a position to create an illustrated talltale video to share with groups of younger students.

Literary Challenge

Two classes create videotapes as methods of discussion about a book or other literary work. Tapes are exchanged as an ongoing dialogue in which students pose questions to each other about the work. Props and costumes are encouraged.

Objectives:

- To stimulate interest in a particular literary work.
- To promote reading for understanding.
- To encourage discourse between students.
- To offer a vehicle for dramatic expression.

Video Equipment and Supplies:

- VCR
- camcorder
- videotapes
- television
- costumes
- markers
- script worksheet on page 75
- paper
- pens and pencils
- books
- stage props
- construction paper
- art supplies as needed

Time: 3–10 hours

Procedure:

1. This is an excellent exercise for pen-pal classes but it works equally well with two classes in the same school. Both classes read the same book or literary work simultaneously. If you are working with another teacher on this project, be sure to create a detailed schedule in advance.

2. At specified points in the story, each class prepares a 3–5 minute videotape that poses specific questions about plot, characterization, or other literary elements and exchanges the tape with the other class, which has prepared a similar tape.

3. When a tape is received, students answer questions thoughtfully and provide support for their ideas from the text. Classes then reply via videotape. Students may choose to use props, wear costumes, assume the roles of characters, create scenery, or use other methods to create an ambiance and provide clues. Scripts are required for each question or answer segment. You may choose to have students use cue cards as well. Encourage students to take turns being actors and technical personnel—encourage style and dramatic license as well.

4. Repeat the exchange of tapes as often as you feel appropriate for the work you select. At the book's conclusion, try to get the classes together for a party in the spirit of the literary work they have shared.

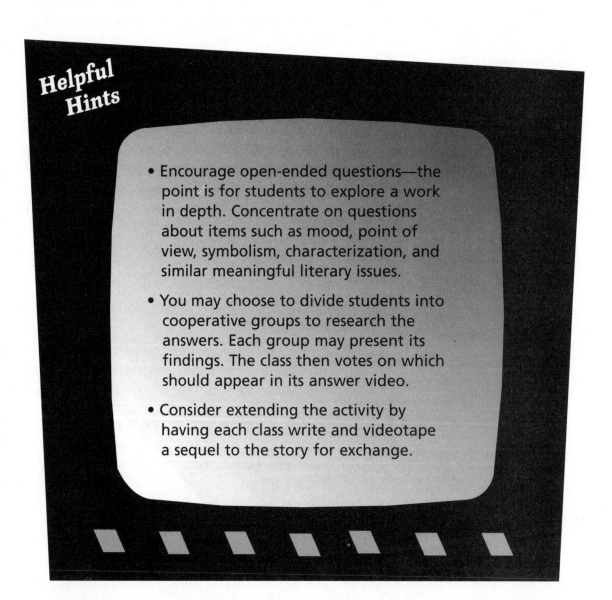

Helpful Hints

- Encourage open-ended questions—the point is for students to explore a work in depth. Concentrate on questions about items such as mood, point of view, symbolism, characterization, and similar meaningful literary issues.

- You may choose to divide students into cooperative groups to research the answers. Each group may present its findings. The class then votes on which should appear in its answer video.

- Consider extending the activity by having each class write and videotape a sequel to the story for exchange.

May I See Your Poetic License?

Students create videotaped presentations of original student poetry.

Objectives:
- To advance interest in poetry and nurture creativity.
- To teach students to write in a concise, descriptive manner.
- To improve public speaking skills.

Video Equipment and Supplies:
- VCR
- camcorder
- videotapes
- television
- paper
- pens and pencils
- costumes
- small props (optional)

Time: 3–5 hours

Procedure:

1. During or after a unit on poetry, encourage students to select a particular poet whose voice inspires or appeals to them and to analyze several of the poet's works for literary elements and content.

2. Invite students to write original poems or collections of poems based on the style or subject matter of the poet they have chosen. They will choose one poem to memorize for videotaping. Dramatic presentations may be enhanced by costumes, small props, or minor sound effects—encourage creative presentations.

3. One student may operate the camcorder as others perform—all may assist with props and sound effects. Record the videographer's poem at the beginning or end of the tape.

4. Share the video with the class before making it available to other classes.

Helpful Hints

- Imaginative presentations can transform this activity from a series of repetitious recitations into an inspiring experience. Encourage creativity repeatedly. For example, a student inspired by Alan Ginsberg might perform with a black turtleneck, sunglasses, black beret, and bongo drums. One student who was touched by Maya Angelou's "Africa" performed her recitation using a simple length of chain for dramatic emphasis— with intense results.

- Consider extending the activity by "publishing" a book containing the original poems to circulate with the video.

Two Minutes With...

Students work in cooperative groups to create videos in which each group member speaks for two minutes about the most important aspects and activities of his or her life. This is a good activity for early in the year.

Objectives:
- To share an activity requiring team effort.
- To provide initial exposure to the operation of a camcorder.
- To provide a safe forum for expression of ideas and opinions.
- To help students get to know one another.

Video Equipment and Supplies:
- VCR
- camcorder
- videotapes
- television
- paper
- construction paper
- pens and pencils
- markers

Time: 3 hours over 2 to 3 days

Procedure:

1. Invite students to individually brainstorm important aspects or activities of their personal lives. Have them choose five to write on construction paper cue cards with markers.

2. Divide students into groups of 4–6. Explain that each group will produce a video in which members speak for two minutes about items on their cue cards. Encourage students to bring small props from home.

3. Set aside time for groups to rehearse prior to the actual taping. Less-confident students may wish to "script" their monologues rather than speak extemporaneously.

4. Be sure each student has an opportunity to operate the camcorder. Plan on each group requiring approximately 20 minutes to complete its tape.

5. When re-recording a flubbed take, turn the VCR/camcorder switch to the *VCR* position to view what you have previously taped (look through the viewfinder or eyepiece). Press *play*, then *rewind*. View the tape as it rewinds, then *pause* immediately before the "bad" take begins. To record the new take, turn the VCR/camcorder button back to the *camcorder* position. After you press *record*, have students wait a few seconds before speaking while the tape gets up to speed. This will ensure that no dialogue is cut off and allow for a bit of extra footage so you can re-record without erasing any quality footage.

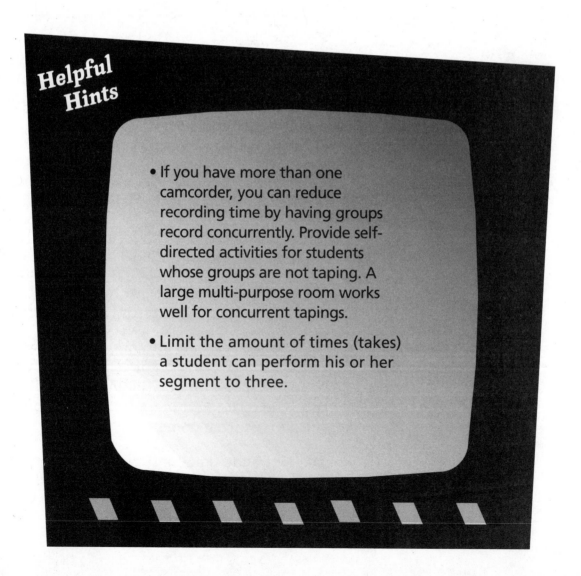

Helpful Hints

• If you have more than one camcorder, you can reduce recording time by having groups record concurrently. Provide self-directed activities for students whose groups are not taping. A large multi-purpose room works well for concurrent tapings.

• Limit the amount of times (takes) a student can perform his or her segment to three.

Video Newspaper

Students produce a videotape in the style of a local news program that highlights important school events of the previous week.

Objectives:
- To promote organizational skills.
- To encourage students to keep abreast of local and national news.
- To teach writing in the journalistic style.

Video Equipment and Supplies:
- VCR
- camcorder
- videotapes
- television
- paper
- construction paper
- pens and pencils
- markers
- script and storyboard worksheets on pages 75-76

Time: 5–10 hours

Procedure:

1. Play a videotape of a local news broadcast for the class. Discuss the format of the broadcast and the types of information presented.

2. List important school events for the following week on the board.

3. Divide the class into news crews of 4 to 6 students. Each crew will cover two to three events and produce a one-minute videotaped segment in the style of a news broadcast that highlights the event.

4. Provide time for groups to write the narrative for their segments (lead-in comments, interview questions, explanations of events, lead-out comments).

5. Have each group appoint reporters, camcorder operators, and production assistants. Send individual crews to cover specified events. Reporters desiring to narrate a segment off-camera may stand to the side of the camcorder and speak into its microphone during taping.

6. Designate one videotape on which all footage will be recorded. Be sure tape is cued to proper position before each crew records a new segment to ensure that prized footage is not erased.

7. Encourage students to add graphics, such as titles and credits, by writing them on construction paper and shooting them at close range.

8. When all segments are recorded, share the tape with the class. Critique the tape with an eye to improving presentations the following week. Discuss what works well and what needs improvement. Make the tape available to other classes through the school library.

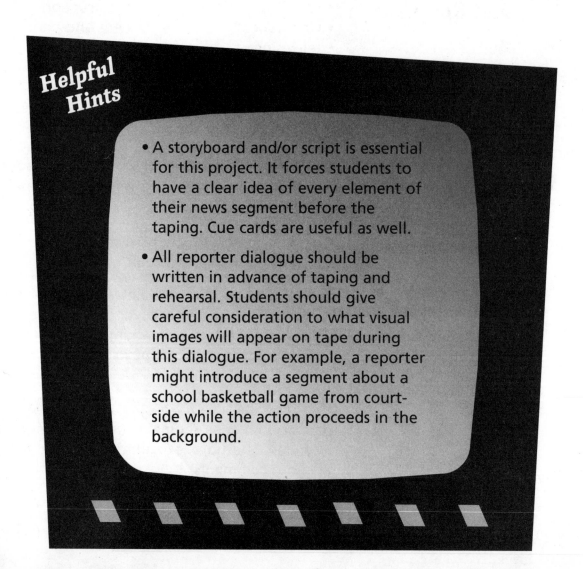

Helpful Hints

- A storyboard and/or script is essential for this project. It forces students to have a clear idea of every element of their news segment before the taping. Cue cards are useful as well.

- All reporter dialogue should be written in advance of taping and rehearsal. Students should give careful consideration to what visual images will appear on tape during this dialogue. For example, a reporter might introduce a segment about a school basketball game from court-side while the action proceeds in the background.

Cultural Perspective

Students produce 3–5 minute videos about their cultural heritages. Interviews, artifacts, and costumes should be included. Students unclear about their ancestries might produce videos about cultures that interest them.

Objectives:

- To acquaint students with the richness and variety of diverse cultures.
- To promote cultural pride among students.
- To provide insight into the background of students.

Video Equipment and Supplies:

- VCR
- camcorder
- videotapes
- television
- family artifacts
- construction paper
- script worksheet on page 75
- paper
- photographs
- pens and pencils
- markers
- audiotapes
- CDs

Time:

4–6 hours

Procedure:

1. Schedule visits to the school or community library—this will enable students to do research that may yield background information for their videos. Suggest that students interview friends and family for anecdotes and local color.

2. Encourage students to brainstorm ideas for their individual videos and create scripts from their best ideas (see sample on page 19). Each script should chronicle all segments of the video and note the duration of each scene.

3. Remind students to highlight cultural aspects they find important and interesting. Encourage them to include artwork, native performing arts, foods, and other unique features of the culture.

4. Assign students to production teams of 3–6 people who will assist each other with such tasks as operating the camcorder and holding cue cards. Remind them to rehearse before shooting.

5. For maximum artistic flexibility, encourage students to shoot footage outside of school if a camcorder is available. Other students will require use of the school camcorder. Develop a sign-up schedule for these students to ensure equal access.

6. To keep interest high, plan to show finished tapes at various specified times, rather than in one marathon showing.

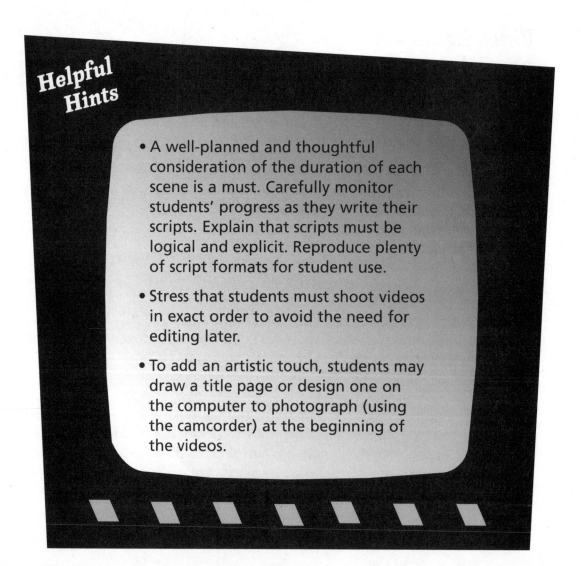

Helpful Hints

• A well-planned and thoughtful consideration of the duration of each scene is a must. Carefully monitor students' progress as they write their scripts. Explain that scripts must be logical and explicit. Reproduce plenty of script formats for student use.

• Stress that students must shoot videos in exact order to avoid the need for editing later.

• To add an artistic touch, students may draw a title page or design one on the computer to photograph (using the camcorder) at the beginning of the videos.

Cultural Perspective

Students produce 3–5 minute videos about their cultural heritages. Interviews, artifacts, and costumes should be included. Students unclear about their ancestries might produce videos about cultures that interest them.

Objectives:

- To acquaint students with the richness and variety of diverse cultures.

- To promote cultural pride among students.

- To provide insight into the background of students.

Video Equipment and Supplies:

- VCR
- camcorder
- videotapes
- television
- family artifacts
- construction paper
- script worksheet on page 75

- paper
- photographs
- pens and pencils
- markers
- audiotapes
- CDs

Time:

4–6 hours

Procedure:

1. Schedule visits to the school or community library—this will enable students to do research that may yield background information for their videos. Suggest that students interview friends and family for anecdotes and local color.

2. Encourage students to brainstorm ideas for their individual videos and create scripts from their best ideas (see sample on page 19). Each script should chronicle all segments of the video and note the duration of each scene.

3. Remind students to highlight cultural aspects they find important and interesting. Encourage them to include artwork, native performing arts, foods, and other unique features of the culture.

4. Assign students to production teams of 3–6 people who will assist each other with such tasks as operating the camcorder and holding cue cards. Remind them to rehearse before shooting.

5. For maximum artistic flexibility, encourage students to shoot footage outside of school if a camcorder is available. Other students will require use of the school camcorder. Develop a sign-up schedule for these students to ensure equal access.

6. To keep interest high, plan to show finished tapes at various specified times, rather than in one marathon showing.

Helpful Hints

- A well-planned and thoughtful consideration of the duration of each scene is a must. Carefully monitor students' progress as they write their scripts. Explain that scripts must be logical and explicit. Reproduce plenty of script formats for student use.

- Stress that students must shoot videos in exact order to avoid the need for editing later.

- To add an artistic touch, students may draw a title page or design one on the computer to photograph (using the camcorder) at the beginning of the videos.

Sample Script

Scene	Audio	Video	Time
1	Hi! My name is Enrique Escobar and I would like to tell you a little bit about my cultural heritage. My family is originally from Guadalajara, Mexico.	Begin with medium close-up of me talking into camcorder. Zoom in to map of Mexico.	:15
2	My great-grandfather and great-grandmother moved to southern California in the mid-1800s. My grandfather first worked in a restaurant cleaning tables but by the time he was 25 years old, he was able to start his own restaurant. It was called *La Cocina Guadalajara,* which means The Guadalajara Kitchen, in honor of where he was born.	Close-up of family portrait of great-grandfather and great-grandmother. Cut to family photo of restaurant.	:30
3	Even though my family has been in the United States for close to 150 years, the culture of Mexico is still very important to us. We eat more traditional Mexican food than we do American food. My father loves the paintings of Mexican artists Diego Rivera and his wife, Frida Kahlo. Traditional Mexican music is popular at my house. (mariachi record plays in background)	Medium shot of me in front of Mexican flag. Cut to shot of family at dinner table eating carnitas with black beans and rice. Cut to close-up of art by Rivera. Cut to close-up of art by Kahlo. End with medium shot of me holding album cover.	:45
4	Spanish and English are both spoken in my house. My mother insists that we speak and read both languages fluently. Here are some examples of Spanish expressions and their meanings in English.	Medium shot of Mom and me.	:30

Distance Debate

Two classes debate a contemporary social issue, such as capital punishment. Each class shoots segments that argue either pros or cons of the issue. Segments are exchanged at regular intervals. Student opinions are tallied at the conclusion of the debate.

Objectives:

- To teach students to analyze different sides of a political or social issue.

- To promote discussion of contemporary social issues.

- To teach students to assume the role of proponent or opponent of a topic of debate.

Video Equipment and Supplies:

- VCR
- camcorder
- videotapes
- television
- reference books and periodicals
- script worksheet on page 75

- paper
- construction paper
- pens and pencils
- markers

Time:

5–10 hours

Procedure:

1. Select a contemporary topic for debate. Designate one class as proponents of the issue and another as opponents.

2. Hold discussions in both classes to consider the topic from all points of view. Appoint student recorders to document important points for reading back to the class at the conclusion of the discussion. Points in support of the class's position may be written on the board.

3. Divide students into the following groups: writers, who compose a persuasive script stating the class position; support personnel, who complete and hold cue cards, position on-screen personnel, and similar tasks; art directors, who design and draw charts, graphs, or other graphics; on-screen personnel, who present the class position; and technical personnel, who shoot the video. Appoint a student director, if you wish, who may also make production decisions and monitor progress.

4. Have each class shoot a 3–5 minute video stating its position. Allow time for several takes. Review the video with students before forwarding it to the opposing class. If another teacher is involved, set a forwarding date in advance.

5. Review the video from the opposing class. Invite volunteers to act as recorders of pertinent points for post-viewing discussion. Following the original procedure, shoot a short rebuttal tape to send the other class. Encourage students to assume different roles for the second shoot. Conduct a secret vote to ascertain which view has the most supporters.

Helpful Hints

- It is important that the technical staff be familiar with the script so it can follow the dialogue smoothly from student to student. It is effective to begin the video with a wide shot and slowly zoom in for a close-up.

- Experiment with camera angles. For example, shooting from slightly below eye level gives an authoritative on-screen presence.

- On-line computer networks, such as the Internet and CompuServe, are excellent meeting places for teachers and students wishing to exchange videos for a project like as this one. See page 78 for a list of forums in which to make connections.

Do You Want My Job?

Pairs of students choose occupations they find interesting and shoot videos highlighting facets of the vocations and people who are engaged in them.

Objectives:

- To encourage students to contemplate future career options.

- To expose students to the realities of various occupations.

- To inform students of the prerequisites and training required for certain vocations.

Video Equipment and Supplies:

- VCR
- camcorder
- videotapes
- television
- paper
- pens and pencils
- script and storyboard worksheets on pages 75-76

Time: Varies

Procedure:

1. Ask students to submit a list of three occupations that interest them and that are accessible in terms of research. Form pairs based on common interests. Each pair will shoot a five-minute video that highlights an occupation. In the case of an odd number of students, inquire at the outset if someone would prefer to work alone.

2. Explain that the videos should include interviews with people actually engaged in the professions and footage of them in action. It will be the students' responsibility to contact these people and arrange interviews.

3. Have students prepare outlines or storyboards of the videos as well as the narrative and interview questions. This will help them explain the project to people who have agreed to be taped.

4. Students may make their own arrangements for traveling to the site of the taping. One student acts as videographer while the other acts as reporter/narrator. Students may alternate assignments during the course of the video, if they choose.

5. If your guidance department sponsors a career day, offer the tapes as part of the presentation. Share them with the class as well. If only one camcorder is available, the project may take place over several months. Encourage the use of family camcorders where possible.

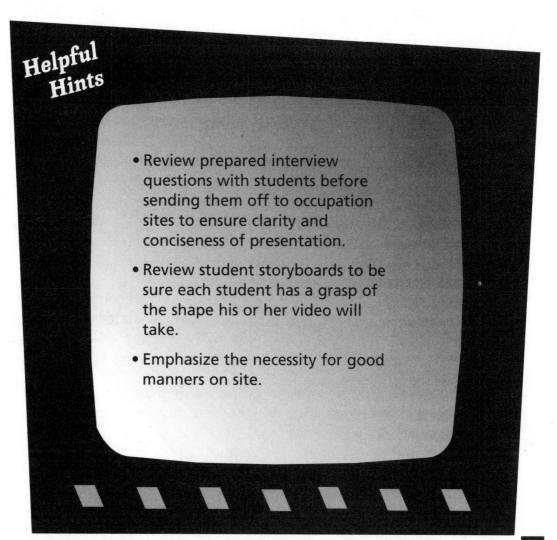

Helpful Hints

- Review prepared interview questions with students before sending them off to occupation sites to ensure clarity and conciseness of presentation.

- Review student storyboards to be sure each student has a grasp of the shape his or her video will take.

- Emphasize the necessity for good manners on site.

Making Television History

Cooperative groups of 4 to 6 students will produce 5–10 minute video summaries of historical events in investigative journalism style.

Objectives:

- To present history in a manner that is relevant and enticing.
- To enhance creative writing skills.
- To develop research skills.
- To foster good communications skills.

Video Equipment and Supplies:

- VCR
- camcorder
- videotapes
- television
- classroom art supplies
- pre-recorded tape of *60 Minutes* or *20/20*
- script and storyboard worksheets on pages 75-76
- paper
- history texts
- pens and pencils
- reference books

Time: 5–10 hours

Procedure:

1. Explain the nature of the assignment and brainstorm a list of historical events students have studied (with you or in the past) that would work well for this project.

2. Play a pre-recorded portion of *60 Minutes* or *20/20*. Have students take notes about program structure as they watch and discuss what they have observed at the conclusion of the tape.

3. Form groups of 4 to 6 students based on their interest in the historical events you have listed. Plan to hold at least one full class in your school library for research. Students may create outlines or lists of main points their videos will cover.

4. Invite groups to write scripts based on their outlines and other research. In the scripts, an investigative reporter will uncover these main points using techniques similar to those utilized in the TV clip (see sample script on page 26).

5. Groups will proceed to make storyboards based on their scripts. Each of the key historical points presented should be accompanied by a visual such as a picture, drawing, costume, artifact, or dramatic enactment, that dramatizes the point. These should be indicated on the storyboards. Allocate class time for creation of the visuals and cue cards, if needed.

6. Have each group designate an investigative reporter. Other group members will share production tasks and appear as featured historical characters. Provide plenty of rehearsal time. Circulate through the groups to provide guidance and suggestions.

7. Create a shooting schedule and be sure students adhere to it. Share completed videos with the class.

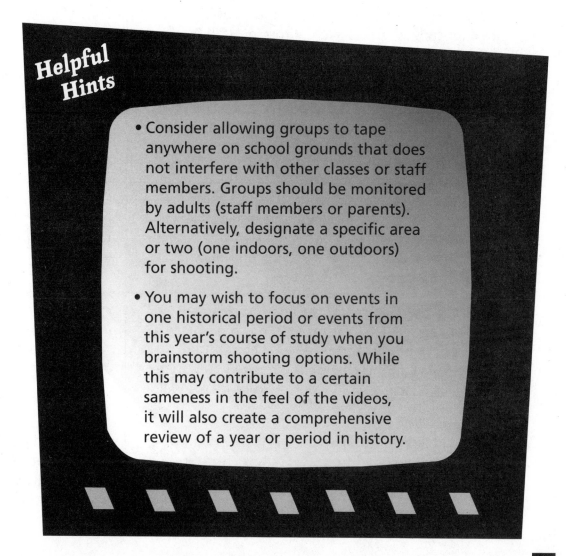

Helpful Hints

- Consider allowing groups to tape anywhere on school grounds that does not interfere with other classes or staff members. Groups should be monitored by adults (staff members or parents). Alternatively, designate a specific area or two (one indoors, one outdoors) for shooting.

- You may wish to focus on events in one historical period or events from this year's course of study when you brainstorm shooting options. While this may contribute to a certain sameness in the feel of the videos, it will also create a comprehensive review of a year or period in history.

Sample Script: Westward Migration

Scene	Audio	Video
1	What would it take to make you leave your home, your friends, your family, and move to a strange new land? During the 1800s in America, that is precisely what thousands of Americans did. They left the eastern United States and headed west for the promise of a better life. I am Jane Phillips and I will try to shed some light on this western migration to see why anyone would heed the cry of "Westward Ho!"	Medium shot of Jane in front of map of North America.
2	Part of the mystery can be unraveled in ads like this one. It proclaims, "Free land for all settlers—1800 acres. A climate so mild that you won't need blankets in the winter." Newspapers, magazines, and books lured thousands of Americans to places like California, Utah, and Texas with ads like this one promising a better life in a new and unspoiled land.	Close-up of student-drawn advertisement for free land in Texas.
3	Thousands of settlers believed ads like the one you have just seen and headed west for a region with fertile farmlands and huge grassy plains—a region called Texas.	Close-up of photo of Texas plains.
4	Texas was once a part of the Spanish colony of Mexico. In 1821, Mexico won its independence from Spain and Texas became a part of Mexican territory that included a vast portion of what is now the western United States.	Close-up of map of North America with Mexican territory of 1830s shaded in.
5	At first, the Mexican government welcomed American settlers to Texas, hoping to promote a strong friendship and trade with the United States. But all this changed. We take you now to Texas in the year 1830 where two residents will give you the inside story.	Close-up of Jane Phillips in the middle of grassy area on playground.
	I would like you to meet Amanda McBride, a settler who moved from St. Louis to Texas in 1921. Amanda, tell us what is happening in Texas.	Pan to student dressed in attire of settler in 1800s. Keep shot wide and deep enough to include grass surrounding settler.

Sample Script: Westward Migration

Scene	Audio	Video
	Amanda: Well, Jane, things were great when I first settled here in 1921. There was plenty of land and the Mexican government left us alone. But things changed. First, they outlawed slavery. Then they outlawed American settlements altogether. We outnumber the Mexicans 4 to 1 in Texas and they are telling us we can't live here. The settlers aren't going to pack up and leave. We will fight for our homes!	
	Jane: The Mexican inhabitants of Texas have a different view. Meet Felipe Montoya. Felipe, what do you think of the American settlers in Texas?	Pan back to Jane.
	Felipe: Jane, the Americans are trying to take over our country. We fought the Spaniards to gain our independence. My relatives died in the struggle. Texas is a part of Mexico and will always be a part of Mexico. We defeated the Spanish and we will defeat the Americans if we have to!	Pan to close-up of student dressed in traditional Mexican attire of 1800s.
6	**Jane:** The tension between American settlers and the Mexican government became so bad that the settlers set up their own government. General Lopez de Santa Anna sent thousands of Mexican soldiers to attack an old mission in San Antonio known as the Alamo. The battle began on February 24, 1836. About 200 Americans were killed, including Davey Crockett and Jim Bowie. *Jane continues to describe the battle of the Alamo, using the model for illustration purposes.* *The remainder of the chapter is investigated in the same style.*	Medium close-up of student model of Alamo.

Meet the Past

Panels of "journalists" will conduct roundtable interviews of America's "founding fathers." Interview questions and answers are based on student research.

Objectives:

- To encourage students to formulate well-reasoned opinions about causes of notable events in U.S. history.

- To bring historical figures to life—to give them interest and relevance.

- To encourage students to formulate their own well-grounded interpretations of history.

- To promote research skills.

Video Equipment and Supplies:

- VCR
- camcorder
- videotapes
- television
- pre-recorded segment of *Meet the Press*
- paper
- pens and pencils
- costumes
- classroom art supplies

Time: 5–10 hours

Procedure:

1. Show a pre-recorded segment of *Meet the Press* to students and discuss the format, which students will follow for this project. List the founding fathers on the board.

2. Divide students into cooperative groups of 4 to 6. Invite groups to select founding fathers to research or assign one to each group. One student from the group will portray the founding father for the project, one will operate the camcorder, and others will act as members of the press. Students not wishing to appear in the video may handle off-camera production duties.

3. Allocate class time in your school library for students to research their founding fathers, making a list of key events and decisions in their lives. These items will be used to formulate three to five questions for "journalists" to ask. For example, a question for Thomas Jefferson might be, "Why did the Federalist Party, and Alexander Hamilton in particular, disapprove of the Louisiana Purchase?" Groups will discuss their questions and develop thoughtful answers.

4. Be sure groups rehearse their segments prior to shooting. Create a shooting schedule to accommodate each group. Costumes and simple backdrops are effective and should be the responsibility of the students.

5. Share completed videos with the class.

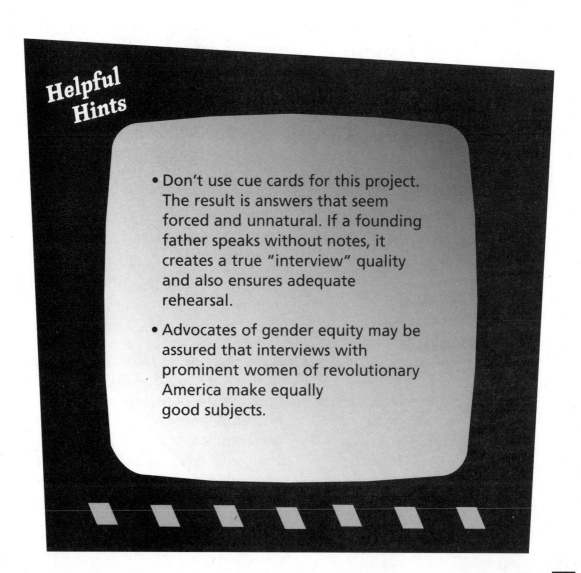

Helpful Hints

- Don't use cue cards for this project. The result is answers that seem forced and unnatural. If a founding father speaks without notes, it creates a true "interview" quality and also ensures adequate rehearsal.

- Advocates of gender equity may be assured that interviews with prominent women of revolutionary America make equally good subjects.

Video Travelogue

Each student creates a promotional video designed to encourage tourists to travel to a country of the student's choice.

Objectives:

- To inspire interest in the culture and history of another country.

- To prompt students to write and speak in persuasive manners.

- To promote organization and problem-solving skills.

Video Equipment and Supplies:

- VCR
- camcorder
- videotapes
- television
- travel brochures
- native costumes
- paper
- pens and pencils
- reference books
- cultural artifacts
- native foods
- crayons or markers
- one or two travel videos (rented)
- script and storyboard worksheets on pages 75-76

Time: 7–10 hours over 2 weeks

Procedure:

1. Explain to students that they have been hired by a travel agency interested in creating a library of travel videos. The 3–5 minute videos must be informative and alluring to tourists.

2. Play one or two travel videos for students. Encourage them to take notes on what they see. Student videos may include historical landmarks, cultural events, prominent geographical features, important people, local color, and recreational opportunities. Pictures of various locales may be shot from travel brochures and books using a camcorder.

3. Invite students to sign up for countries they wish to research. Avoid duplication by encouraging students to have two or three choices in mind. Allocate time for students to do some research in the school library. Your community library will have valuable resources that students should be encouraged to review as well. Have students list possible points of interest as their research progresses. They will ultimately choose seven to ten points to include in their videos.

4. Each student will complete a script and a 10–12 frame storyboard (see page 32) for this project, as well as any cue cards that are necessary. Review scripts and storyboards with students before giving them the go-ahead to shoot. Insist that students adhere to the formats developed in their scripts and storyboards.

5. Form production teams of 3 to 5 students to assist each other with production details. Encourage use of home camcorders and offer the school camcorder on a sign-up basis. Try to offer some after-school time for using the school camcorder.

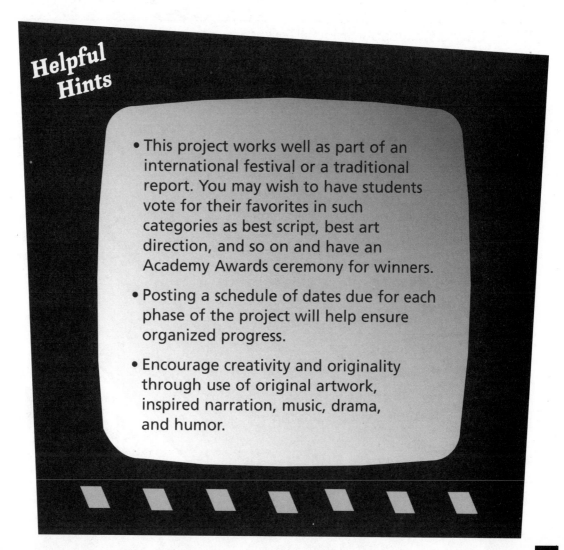

Helpful Hints

- This project works well as part of an international festival or a traditional report. You may wish to have students vote for their favorites in such categories as best script, best art direction, and so on and have an Academy Awards ceremony for winners.

- Posting a schedule of dates due for each phase of the project will help ensure organized progress.

- Encourage creativity and originality through use of original artwork, inspired narration, music, drama, and humor.

Sample Storyboard

Scene	Description	Picture	Time
1	Video segment of student sitting at travel agent's desk examining travel brochures. *I need a vacation desperately.*		:20
2	Cut to still image of bullet train. *But I don't want to be stuck in one spot. I want to see lots of new and exciting places.*		:10
3	Cut to still image of Eiffel Tower followed by Arch de Triomphe. *It has to be elegant. I have to be surrounded by grace and beauty.*		:15
4	Cut to still image of "Mona Lisa" followed by Monet's "Waterlilies" followed by Rodin's "The Thinker." *I want to wander through rooms filled with celebrated paintings and sculpture.*		:15
5	Cut to video segment of student in garden. *I want to sip cocoa and have breakfast in a beautiful garden.* And so on.		:10

Running Time: __1:10__

Brighter Colors
and Whiter
Whites

A pinwheel containing all the colors of the spectrum is rotated to produce white light, thus demonstrating that white is actually a combination of all colors. The experiment is broadcast through a television connected to a camcorder.

Objectives:

- To demonstrate that white light is a combination of all the colors of the spectrum.

- To heighten student interest in principles of light and color.

- To encourage students to hypothesize why a spinning rainbow-colored disc appears white.

Video Equipment and Supplies:

- VCR
- camcorder
- videotapes
- television
- phonograph turntable or portable drill
- phono cable
- tripod (if available)
- paper
- pens and pencils
- tempera paints
- paintbrush
- flashlight
- prism
- paper plate
- ruler

Time: 1–2 hours

Procedure:

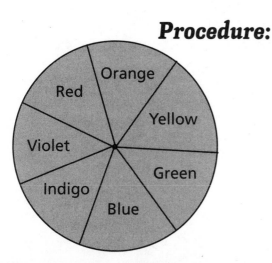

1. Cut a paper plate into a circle with a diameter between 6" and 10" (15 cm and 25 cm). Divide the circle into seven equal segments and paint each segment to correspond precisely with the diagram. The order of colors must match. The colors represent the colors of the visible light spectrum (the colors of the rainbow).

2. Connect a camcorder to a VCR that is connected to a television, following the diagram on page 36. Turn the camcorder, television, and VCR on. You will need to push the *Input Selection* button on the VCR to switch it to the *line in* position. This will allow images from the camcorder to flow straight to the television. You may also need to push the *TV/Video* button to put the VCR in video mode.

3. Aim the camcorder at the turntable and view the television to be sure the turntable appears on the television. Refer to page 35 if you have a problem.

4. Once you have tested your video equipment and completed the spectrum wheel, you are ready to begin the lesson. Shine a flashlight through a prism against a white surface. Invite students to describe what they see. Encourage them to name the colors.

5. Display the spectrum wheel and point out that it contains all the colors of the visible light spectrum—the colors just viewed through the prism.

6. Place the spectrum wheel on the turntable so the center post pokes through the center of the wheel. If you are using a drill, poke the drill bit through the center of the wheel so that the colors are facing away from the body of the drill. Have a student aim the camcorder at the turntable or drill and zoom in for a close-up of the spectrum wheel. Invite students to speculate about what they will see when the wheel begins to rotate.

7. Turn the phonograph to its fastest speed (78 rpm) or turn on the drill and televise the event for the class. The spinning spectrum wheel will appear white.

8. Turn off the phonograph or drill and invite students to offer explanations for what they have seen on the TV screen. When the spectrum wheel spun at a high speed, students' eyes blended the colors together and saw white. Be sure students understand that white light is a combination of the colors of the visible spectrum.

Troubleshooting

Do not despair if you cannot get your camcorder to send signals to the television—it is a minor problem. Broadcasting live to a television is a technique you will find countless uses for once you have mastered it. Hang in there!

1. Be sure you have a standard phono cable as shown in the diagram on page 36. Plug one end of this cable into the *video out* jack on your camcorder. Plug the other end of the cable into the *video in* jack on your VCR. This will ensure that the video signal (picture) travels from your camcorder to the VCR.

2. Be sure your VCR is connected to a television.

3. Be sure your television is tuned into the correct channel (3 or 4) to allow the VCR to work in conjunction with it.

4. Your VCR probably has a button marked *TV/Video* or *VCR/TV*. Push the button until the word *video* or *VCR* appears in the display on the front of the VCR.

5. If you have completed the preceding four steps successfully and you are still not seeing images from the camcorder on your television, there is one button on your VCR that may require pushing. It has a variety of names—on the Mitsubishi VCR it is called *input select.* It may also be called *line in* or *source in*. This button tells the VCR that you are sending an external video signal (picture from the camcorder) into the VCR. The VCR accepts these signals and sends them on to the television. Push this button until EXT (external) appears in the display on the front of the VCR. Or, on JVC VCRs, select channel 0—AUX will appear on the display.

6. If you are still not succeeding, find the student in your school who is the resident A/V techno-whiz. Every school has one. He or she will happily rectify the problem in a matter of minutes. You may also call a store that carries your brand/model of VCR for technical assistance. As a last resort, consult the manual. Look under "recording from another source."

7. Some televisions allow you to run phono cables straight from the VCR into the television (these are often referred to as "television monitors" or simply "monitors"). They allow you to bypass the VCR altogether.

Camcorder Connection to VCR

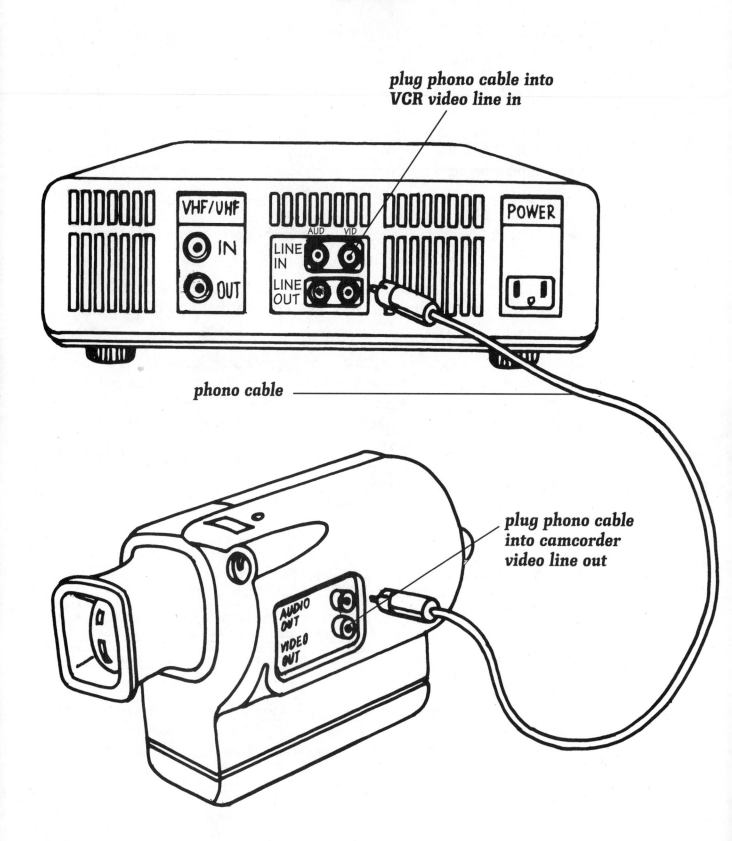

plug phono cable into
VCR video line in

VHF/VHF
IN
OUT

AUD   VID
LINE IN
LINE OUT

POWER

phono cable

plug phono cable
into camcorder
video line out

AUDIO OUT
VIDEO OUT

Mother Earth Would Be Proud

Pairs of students appear on a single video demonstrating simple ways individuals can help protect the environment.

Objectives:

- To promote student concern for the environment.
- To prompt students to contemplate solutions to environmental problems.
- To strengthen research skills.

Video Equipment and Supplies:

- VCR
- camcorder
- videotapes
- television
- visual aids for student presentations
- script and storyboard worksheets on pages 75-76
- paper
- pens and pencils

Time: 2–3 hours

Procedure:

1. Brainstorm with students a list of specific examples of environmental destruction. List these on the board.

2. Invite students to suggest possible remedies for these examples. Encourage them to postulate a few realistic ways in which they can be part of the remedies. Add these to the board as well.

3. Divide students into pairs. Explain that each pair will demonstrate on video one way in which individuals can help solve our environmental problems. It may be a problem they have listed or one they have not as yet thought of. For example, one pair might choose to deal with the issue of recycling as it promotes fewer landfills and forest preservation. Another might wish to demonstrate composting.

4. Allocate time in the school library for student pairs to research and select an environmental problem to focus on. Alert your media specialist so that he or she can be ready with appropriate periodicals and books. Encourage students to look in the community library as well for books that include activities and information.

5. Have students outline the key points they will discuss or have them write actual scripts. Storyboarding will enable them to focus on the visual aids they will need. Students are responsible for creating their own visual aids.

6. Set a date for shooting the video. Allow adequate time for rehearsal. Student pairs will perform their presentations for the class while assigned videographers tape the proceedings. Offer the tape to other classes, particularly younger students.

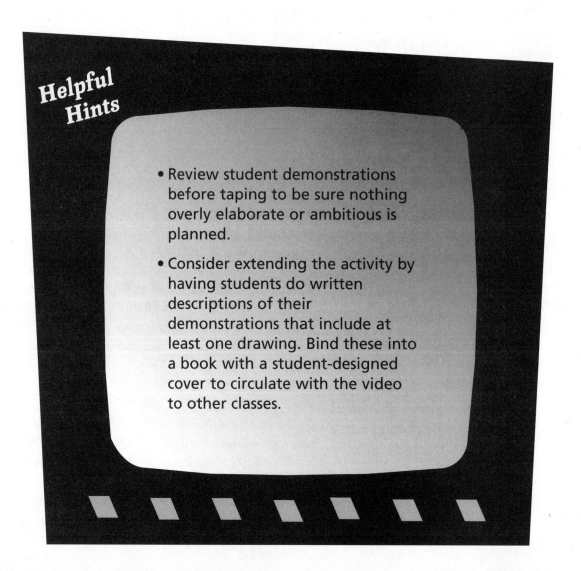

Helpful Hints

- Review student demonstrations before taping to be sure nothing overly elaborate or ambitious is planned.

- Consider extending the activity by having students do written descriptions of their demonstrations that include at least one drawing. Bind these into a book with a student-designed cover to circulate with the video to other classes.

Tally Me Bananas

Students make a time-lapse video of exposed banana slices to dramatize the effects of oxidation over the course of a day.

Objectives:

- To encourage students to offer thoughtful explanations for natural phenomena.

- To invite students to predict the outcome of a scientific experiment.

- To acquaint students with the concept of oxidation.

- To heighten student awareness of the effects of chemical change in common items.

Video Equipment and Supplies:

- VCR
- camcorder
- videotapes
- television
- index cards
- Vitamin C tablet (available at drug, grocery, or health food stores)
- paper
- pens and pencils
- measuring cup
- 1 cup of water
- 2 paper plates
- markers

Time: 6 hours

Procedure:

1. Cut six slices from a banana. Crush the Vitamin C tablet and stir into one cup of water to dissolve. Dip three banana slices into the Vitamin C solution and place on a paper plate. Place the undipped banana slices on a second plate.

2. Write the current time on two index cards along with the words *Vitamin C* or *No Vitamin C.* Position the index cards next to the appropriate plates.

3. Invite students to predict the condition of the six banana slices in five or six hours and write these predictions on paper or in science notebooks.

4. Have a student make a ten-second tape of the banana slices immediately after preparing them. Appoint one or several responsible students to shoot the bananas every half-hour throughout the day. They should write the appropriate time on an index card prior to each shooting.

5. On the following day, play the entire video for the class. Invite students to observe the changes in the banana slices. On prediction papers or in science notebooks, have students describe the changes and note any discrepancies between their predictions and observations.

6. Explain to students that oxygen in the air reacts with materials in fruits in a process called *oxidation.* Vitamin C inhibits oxidation and is called an *antioxidant.* The banana slices dipped in the Vitamin C solution do not turn as brown as the other slices because they do not oxidize as quickly.

Helpful Hints

- Advise students shooting the experiment that permission to tape is not required each time. They are responsible for monitoring the experiment.

- Begin the experiment as early in the day as possible for maximum oxidation.

- Invite students to share predictions and observations. Encourage them to analyze discrepancies between predictions and observations, as well as any other conclusions they may have reached.

- Consider extending the activity by inviting groups of students to videotape a time-lapse sequence of their own design.

Voyage to the Bottom of the Sea

Students simulate underwater exploration via a remote-controlled "robot." Students maneuvering the "robot" see its image only on the television screen.

Objectives:

- To interest students in undersea exploration and help them see parallels between outer space exploration and undersea exploration.

- To promote student concern for the fate of oceans.

- To interest students in the tragic events of ships such as the *Titanic* and *Andrea Doria*.

Video Equipment and Supplies:

- VCR
- camcorder
- phono cable
- television
- paper
- remote-controlled car
- pens and pencils
- tripod
- art and craft supplies as needed to simulate undersea environment

Time: 5–10 hours

Procedure:

1. Discuss with students the limits on exploration imposed by an undersea environment. Compare these limitations with those imposed by outer space. Lead students to an understanding that a remote-controlled robot is useful for exploration and sample-gathering in alien environments, such as outer space or under the sea. Robots are not subject to human constraints, such as the need for oxygen, and can be controlled by humans in safe and comfortable environments.

2. Review the tragic events of the maiden voyage of the RMS *Titanic* in 1912. Share information about the joint French-American expedition led by Jean-Louis Michel and Robert

Ballard that located the wreck on the floor of the Atlantic in 1985. Encourage students to explore details of the subsequent exploration of the *Titanic* in 1986 by Ballard and his crew, paying special attention to the use of the submarine Alvin, and its remote-controlled robot, Jason Junior.

3. Explain that students will build and participate in a simulation that will give them an idea of how it feels to manipulate a robot such as Jason Junior.

4. Divide students into cooperative groups of 4–6. Each group will be responsible for designing and building two or three components of the underwater scene Ballard might have found when he discovered the *Titanic.* Brainstorm with students a complete list of possibilities and invite groups to choose those items that interest them to research and recreate. The scene should include "natural" underwater plant and animal life as well as pieces of the wreck. Set a date by which the scenario must be complete.

5. On the appointed day, help students assemble their "ocean floor" in the hall outside your classroom, in an adjacent classroom, or in a large supply closet, if your room has one. Be sure to have pre-tested the remote-controlled car you will be using so you know the remote power will reach from your classroom to the "bottom of the sea."

6. Once the ocean floor is in place, set the camcorder on a tripod so that it can record the entire scene with a minimum of manipulation. Connect the camcorder via the VCR as detailed on page 36 to the television, which is in your classroom. Students will manipulate the "robot" through the undersea scene according to what they see on the TV monitor. *They will not be able to see the robot directly.* Other students will take turns manipulating the camcorder so the robot operator can follow the robot.

7. You may wish to create an obstacle course for the robot to travel to pick up certain samples. Have each group choose a member to manipulate the robot, one to operate the camcorder, and others to pick up samples as the robot contacts them. Replace the items for each group's turn. Time each group to see which is fastest.

8. An added degree of difficulty may be obtained by placing the videographer on a skateboard rather than having the camcorder on a tripod. A member of the group slowly pushes the skateboard, allowing the videographer to more closely track the robot. This is known as "dollying" and diminishes abrupt camera movement as well as offering a low camera angle.

- You will need a remote-controlled car that goes left and right as well as forward and backward. Check with students or go to an electronics store.

- The following references are fascinating accounts of Ballard's work and of the wreck itself.

Exploring the Titanic by Robert Ballard (Madison Press Books, 1988).

The Discovery of the Titanic by Robert Ballard (Warner Books, 1987).

"A Long Last Look at the Titanic," by Robert Ballard. *National Geographic,* December 1986, p. 698.

Winds of Change

Students make a brief recording of a nearby park, field, or playground each month of the school year to highlight and monitor changes in nature. Students keep journals in which to record monthly observations.

Objectives:

- To generate an appreciation of the natural environment.
- To improve observation skills.
- To dramatize the affects of seasonal changes.
- To promote interest in conservation.

Video Equipment and Supplies:

- VCR
- camcorder
- videotapes
- television
- paper
- journals
- pens and pencils

Time:

1–2 hours per month all year

Procedure:

1. Select a nearby park, field, or playground. Take the class to the selected site and explain that they will be monitoring changes there for the entire year via video.

2. On the first visit, note the date, time, condition of plant life, presence of animals, water level of ponds, and even the presence of litter. Designate a team to shoot a 2 to 3 minute video documenting the initial condition of the site. No narration is necessary. Specify items for recording and keep a list of those items for future shoots (including the same items each time makes for easier viewing of changes).

3. Begin with a panoramic view of the site. Then zoom in on the designated items. Each month during the school year, send a new video team to record changes. All segments should appear in succession on one videotape.

4. Play the entire video each time a segment is added. Discuss with students changes they have witnessed. Encourage them to record their thoughts and observations in a journal. Continue the process throughout the school year.

5. If you wish to extend the activity, invite students to create either poems, illustrations, or both, based on the natural cycles they have observed on the video.

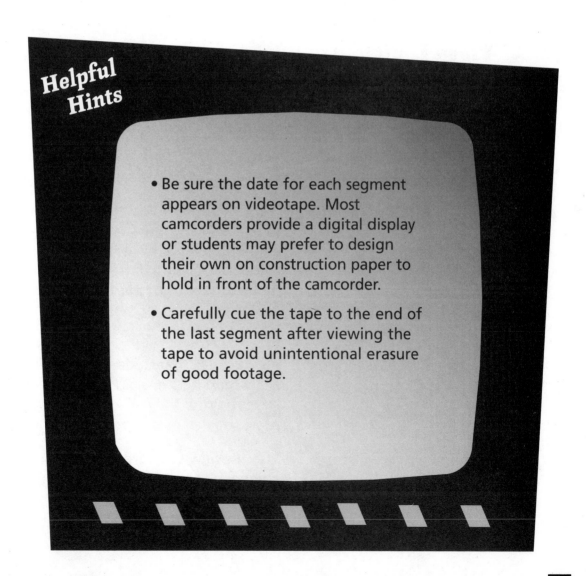

Helpful Hints

- Be sure the date for each segment appears on videotape. Most camcorders provide a digital display or students may prefer to design their own on construction paper to hold in front of the camcorder.

- Carefully cue the tape to the end of the last segment after viewing the tape to avoid unintentional erasure of good footage.

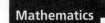

Action Fractions

Students shoot a video explaining fractions to second or third graders. Cooperative groups produce one 5-minute segment each using the students themselves as manipulatives.

Objectives:

- To reinforce understanding of basic concepts in fractions.
- To provide an entertaining and interesting lesson for a class of younger students.
- To gain an appreciation of the teaching process.

Video Equipment and Supplies:

- VCR
- camcorder
- videotapes
- television
- paper
- pens and pencils
- script and storyboard worksheets on pages 75-76

Time: 5–10 hours

Procedure:

1. Invite six volunteers to come up and stand in a row facing their classmates. Discuss with students various ways in which the group of six could be described "fractionally." For example, half of the group is girls, one-third of the group is wearing jeans, or two-thirds of the group has blond hair.

2. Explain that students will use concepts such as these to help explain fractions to students in lower grades. They will work in groups of 3–6 to provide a variety of options for fractions.

3. Review basic fractions. Remind students to emphasize the idea that fractions are parts of a whole—the whole, in this case, being the cooperative group.

4. Encourage creativity and movement. Students may use music, dance, props, or costumes to enliven their show. Distribute script and storyboard worksheets so that students may organize their presentations. Circulate among groups as they develop their lessons.

5. Schedule a day by which scripts and storyboards are to be submitted for your approval, as well as a day for shooting the video. Preview each presentation on the day before shooting for accuracy of concept. Invite students to critique each other's presentations for ease of comprehension and interest level. Appoint two student videographers for the final tape.

6. Consider having a student create a title for the video on construction paper. Invite students to introduce themselves at the end of their respective segments.

7. Share the video with students before offering it to lower-grade classes.

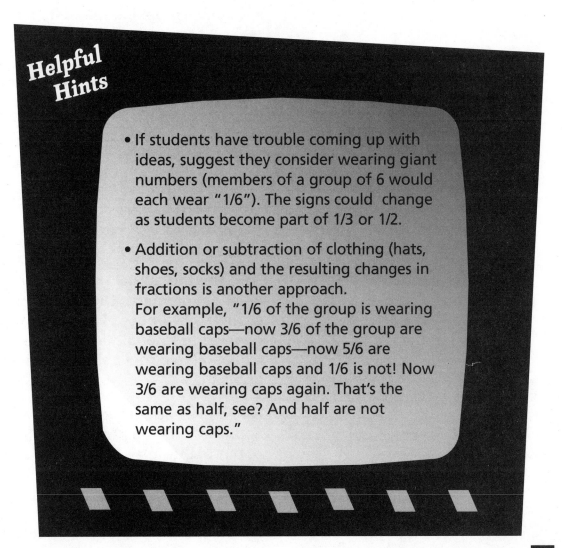

Helpful Hints

- If students have trouble coming up with ideas, suggest they consider wearing giant numbers (members of a group of 6 would each wear "1/6"). The signs could change as students become part of 1/3 or 1/2.

- Addition or subtraction of clothing (hats, shoes, socks) and the resulting changes in fractions is another approach.
  For example, "1/6 of the group is wearing baseball caps—now 3/6 of the group are wearing baseball caps—now 5/6 are wearing baseball caps and 1/6 is not! Now 3/6 are wearing caps again. That's the same as half, see? And half are not wearing caps."

Math-a-Graph

Cooperative groups of 4–6 students shoot 10-minute videos that demonstrate graphing. Students choose school-related topics, decide on appropriate graph forms, render the graphs, and explain them on video.

Objectives:
- To reinforce graphing concepts.
- To relate graphing to everyday events in students' lives.
- To promote cross-tutoring among peers.
- To make graphing relevant and fun.

Video Equipment and Supplies:
- VCR
- camcorder
- videotapes
- television
- posterboard
- compasses
- rulers and yardsticks or meter sticks
- paper
- math texts
- pens and pencils
- construction paper
- calculators
- protractors

Time: 5–7 hours

Procedure:

1. Use this authentic assessment activity after a unit on graphing. Divide students into cooperative groups of 4–6 and invite them to brainstorm among themselves some interesting school-related topics that lend themselves to graphing.

2. Have each group write down, for your approval, one topic from their list and the form of graph they plan to make. To assure a good mix, you may wish to assign graph forms, such as line, bar, or circle, and have students come up with appropriate topics for the graph forms.

3. Once topics and graph forms are approved, allocate class time for students to research their statistics and create their graphs on posterboard. Students might choose topics such as number of girls vs. number of boys participating on school sports teams (double bar graph), absenteeism in their grade compared to other grades over the school year (double or triple line graph), or ethnicity of the student body (circle graph).

4. The videos should begin as students introduce their topics and start their research. Group members may take turns documenting other members as they interview or look up information for the project or students may have assigned roles (videographer, interviewer, statistician, art director).

5. Students should explain on the videos how they made the transition from raw statistics to the graph or *picture* of the statistics. The videos should end with an explanation of student findings as portrayed on their graphs.

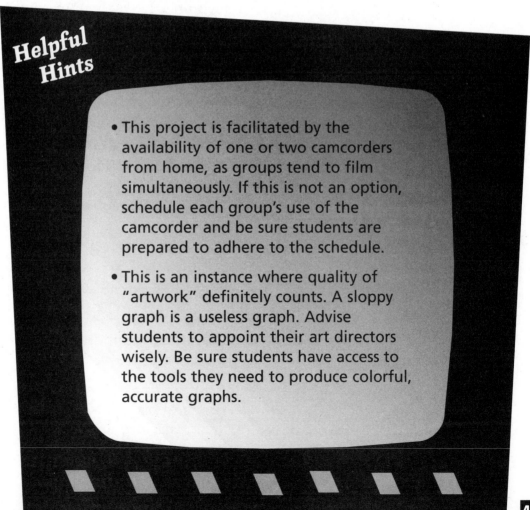

Helpful Hints

- This project is facilitated by the availability of one or two camcorders from home, as groups tend to film simultaneously. If this is not an option, schedule each group's use of the camcorder and be sure students are prepared to adhere to the schedule.

- This is an instance where quality of "artwork" definitely counts. A sloppy graph is a useless graph. Advise students to appoint their art directors wisely. Be sure students have access to the tools they need to produce colorful, accurate graphs.

Real World Math

Teams of students produce 2–3 minute videos highlighting math concepts used in some facet of their everyday lives.

Objectives:

- To demonstrate the relevance and importance of mathematics.
- To promote number sense.
- To reinforce math concepts taught in the classroom.

Video Equipment and Supplies:

- VCR
- camcorder
- videotapes
- television
- art supplies as needed
- script and storyboard worksheets on pages 75-76
- paper
- math texts
- pens and pencils
- construction paper

Time: Varies

Procedure:

1. Teams of students brainstorm real-world examples of classroom math topics that appear in their daily lives—for example, the use of percentages when items go on sale ; the use of fractions in dividing a pizza; the volume of soft drinks sold at the local diner; the use of triangles in framing a new house. The team selects a topic to feature in its video.

2. Scripts and/or storyboards are prepared to organize the presentations. Props and cue cards are provided as needed.

3. As an example, a group might purchase a lottery ticket, record the transaction, and calculate the probability of their winning the various prizes. Another example might be based on rounding off and adding in order not to spend more than one's allotted cash at the supermarket. Students make logistical arrangements and secure any required permissions for taping. Production tasks are delegated to individual team members.

4. Teams rehearse scenes before shooting. Because much of the work is done outside of school, you may wish to use this as an extra credit assignment.

5. Students travel to designated locations and shoot their videos. Completed tapes are shared with the class.

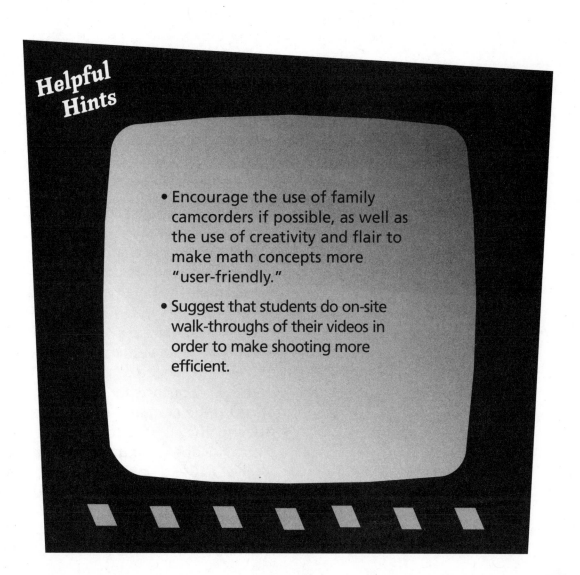

Helpful Hints

- Encourage the use of family camcorders if possible, as well as the use of creativity and flair to make math concepts more "user-friendly."

- Suggest that students do on-site walk-throughs of their videos in order to make shooting more efficient.

The Math Shopping Network

Students create videos in the style of the Home Shopping Network that reinforce math concepts in the context of making a sale.

Objectives:
- To demonstrate practical math applications.
- To relieve math anxiety.
- To encourage students to use math skills to solve real-life problems.

Video Equipment and Supplies:
- VCR
- camcorder
- videotapes
- television
- paper
- pens and pencils
- calculators (optional)
- costumes
- pre-recorded segment of *The Home Shopping Network* or *QVC*.
- mock products (brought from home)

Time: 5–8 hours

Procedure:

1. Play a pre-recorded segment of *The Home Shopping Network* or similar channel. Explain that the project is to parody the program while, at the same time, involve current math concepts. For example, bring a cooked pizza to class and inform students that you have created the new nuclear Mega-Pizza, available only from the *Math Shopping Network*. Talk about the taste and nutritive value of the pizza. Tell students that the pizza costs ten cents per square inch. Measure the diameter of the pizza and tell students they'll have to calculate the cost of one pizza. Anyone pricing the pizza correctly will receive a 10% discount, provided that he or she can quote the discount and the discounted price. Cut the pizza into eight slices and invite students to calculate the price of each slice.

2. Divide students into cooperative groups of 4–6. You may assign specific math topics and/or skills or have students select their own. Groups will brainstorm ideas for style and format.

3. Have groups complete scripts and/or storyboards prior to shooting. Math problems for classmates to solve must be part of the script and must be calculated correctly by each group before presentations. Groups begin rehearsing once their scripts, storyboards, and mathematical calculations have been approved.

4. Create a shooting schedule. Props and costumes are the responsibility of each student. Groups are allowed a maximum of three takes.

5. When videos are completed, distribute paper so students can calculate answers as required for each video. Play the videos, pausing for students to calculate as math problems are presented. Or consider having groups write out their math problems on separate worksheets. This allows you to play the videos straight through, distribute the worksheets, and have students do the math all at once.

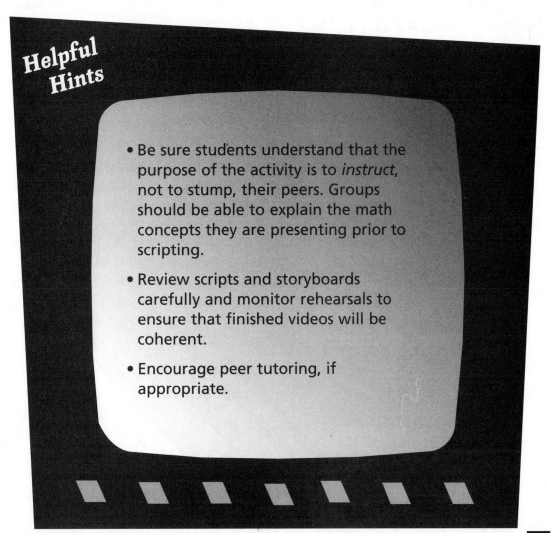

Helpful Hints

- Be sure students understand that the purpose of the activity is to *instruct*, not to stump, their peers. Groups should be able to explain the math concepts they are presenting prior to scripting.

- Review scripts and storyboards carefully and monitor rehearsals to ensure that finished videos will be coherent.

- Encourage peer tutoring, if appropriate.

And Now, a Word from Our Sponsor

Students work in cooperative groups to create videotaped television commercials promoting products of their choice. Each group is responsible for creating an original product, logo, and slogan.

Objectives:
- To view advertising in a discerning and analytical manner.
- To develop a persuasive writing style.
- To advocate student participation in the dramatic arts.

Video Equipment and Supplies:
- VCR
- camcorder
- videotapes
- television
- classroom art supplies
- pre-recorded tape of 10–12 diverse television commercials
- script and storyboard worksheets on pages 75-76
- paper
- pens and pencils
- construction paper
- markers
- list of slogans

Time: 5–10 hours

Procedure:

1. Show a tape of television commercials to the class. Pause the tape after each commercial to discuss aspects such as target audience and method (bandwagon, image, testimonial, informational, the good life, keeping up with the Joneses, and so on).

2. Invite students to comment on which commercials they prefer and why. Mention that in a 30-second commercial, advertisers have only 6 or 7 seconds in which to grab and hold their audience's attention. Discuss some ways they have done this on the tape. Ask how many times the product's name is seen or heard in the course of the commercial and when.

3. Explain logos and slogans. Invite students to identify the logos or slogans you have selected or volunteer a few of their own. What makes the slogans memorable (or not)?

4. Divide students into cooperative groups of 4–6. Each group is to create a new product, a logo, a slogan, and interesting packaging.

5. Once the products are complete, have students write scripts and/or storyboards for one-minute television commercials. Remind them to keep their target audience in mind. Encourage use of music as well as other creative options. Review completed scripts or storyboards with students before they begin production.

6. Have groups use cue cards if necessary. Allocate plenty of rehearsal time. Schedule a date for final shooting and establish a maximum number of takes allowable.

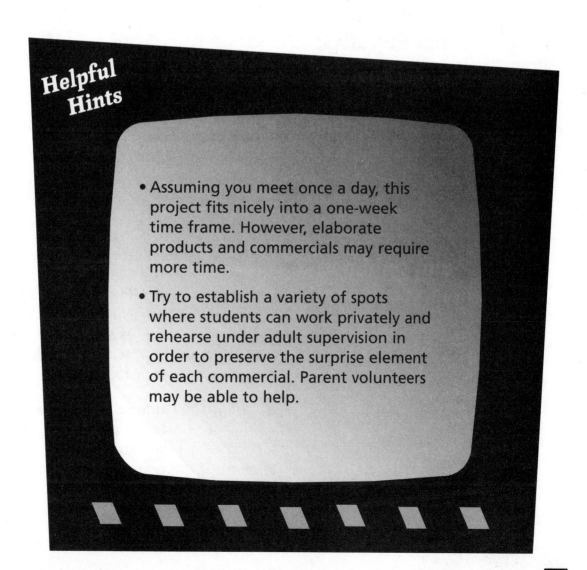

Helpful Hints

- Assuming you meet once a day, this project fits nicely into a one-week time frame. However, elaborate products and commercials may require more time.

- Try to establish a variety of spots where students can work privately and rehearse under adult supervision in order to preserve the surprise element of each commercial. Parent volunteers may be able to help.

Critic's Corner

A song usually begins as a poem. Students work in pairs to review the music and lyrics of artists of their choice, with an emphasis on the poems that shape the original songs.

Objectives:

- To provoke thoughtful analysis of music and lyrics.

- To teach students to appreciate differing opinions.

- To refine persuasive writing skills.

Video Equipment and Supplies:

- VCR
- camcorder
- videotapes
- television
- CDs or cassettes
- music reviews from *Rolling Stone* or *People* Magazine
- printed copies of sample lyrics
- paper
- pens and pencils
- markers
- construction paper

Time: 4–6 hours

Procedure:

1. Share one or two CD/cassette reviews with students. Have the CDs available as well as copies of the lyrics. Play some of the songs mentioned in the review. Discuss the opinions of the reviewers and ways in which they are presented and justified. Ask students what they think the purpose of a review is.

2. Engage students in a discussion about the lyrics of a selected popular song. Read the poem aloud or invite a volunteer to read it. Ask students if the poem stands alone, apart from the music. Does the music add or detract from the poem? How?

3. Invite students to bring in CDs or cassettes that include printed lyrics appropriate for school. Students may bring in CDs they like or dislike. You may wish to supply a few of your own, such as music by James Taylor, Carole King, the Beatles, or Paul Simon—all of whom set their own poetry to music. Make copies of lyrics.

4. Invite pairs of students to select CDs or cassettes containing songs with lyrics and music they enjoy. Explain that students will write and videotape reviews of the CDs or cassettes. The reviews should focus on the lyrics and music of one or two particular selections. Cue cards, if used, should not include the entire review.

5. Remind students that unsupported opinions are unacceptable. Set a date on which you will critique written reviews before allowing students to begin shooting.

6. If possible, arrange for a location outside the classroom where students may shoot the video. Prepare a simple setting, such as two chairs behind a desk in front of an appropriate backdrop. Invite one student to operate the camcorder and two to handle cue cards. Rotate these roles as you see fit.

Helpful Hints

- If students wish to include music in their reviews, it is important that CDs be cued properly before reviews are taped. You may wish to limit students to one such item.

- Keep in mind that popular music is an enormous source of inspiration for students. This lesson may seem unorthodox, but it can often launch some highly creative and analytical writing.

- Consider extending the activity by inviting students to debate which is the more important element of a popular song, the music or the lyrics.

Karaoke TV

Students work in cooperative groups to write new lyrics to familiar tunes, using karaoke tapes. Songs become part of a music video.

Objectives:

- To highlight the joy of singing.
- To give students an appreciation of the song-writing process.
- To give relevance to the poetry-writing process.
- To encourage creativity.

Video Equipment and Supplies:

- VCR
- camcorder
- videotapes
- television
- cassette player
- karaoke tapes
- storyboard worksheets on page 76
- paper
- pens and pencils
- costumes
- classroom art supplies

Time: 7–10 hours

Procedure:

1. Ask students if they are familiar with the term *karaoke* and its derivation. Explain to students that karaoke originated in Japanese nightclubs—the word *karaoke* means *empty orchestra.* Karaoke tapes feature music tracks of popular songs without vocals, thus allowing people to sing along.

2. Divide students into groups of 4 to 6. Explain that they will work with karaoke tapes and their own lyrics to create original music videos. Students may acquire their own karaoke tapes or use a tape that you make available. Set a date by which all tapes must be in school.

3. You may wish to decide collectively on a theme for lyrics, such as environmental preservation or another social issue, or you may choose to have students select their own. Remind students to avoid tired clichés and write with thoughtfulness and good taste. Establish a due date for lyrics, which you will approve before students move ahead.

4. Once lyrics are approved, students will design a presentation for their songs. Costumes, props, lighting, and sets may all be utilized. Limit students to a 30-minute presentation. MTV-type camera work, such as weird angles and jittery cameras, are perfectly acceptable, as long as they make artistic sense and are not simply gratuitous experiments.

5. Storyboards will help students organize their presentations. Schedule a review of completed storyboards and group concepts. Allocate plenty of rehearsal time. Lyrics should be memorized and clearly articulated by singers. Movements should be choreographed.

6. Closely monitor groups as they make their videos. Before shooting begins, adjust the volume of the karaoke tape to match the volume of the singing group (have them sing a few bars). Arrange a gala presentation of the finished music videos. Consider a music video award ceremony as a finale.

Helpful Hints

- Remember that style is the main issue on MTV—sequence and story line are secondary. Relax, enjoy, and give your left brain a rest.

- Sources for karaoke tapes:

  The Singing Machine Co., Inc.
  6350 E. Rogers Circle
  Boca Raton, Florida 33487

  Priddis Music Corporation
  1030 W. 500 North
  Lindon, UT 84042-1123
  (801) 785-6666

  Backtrax Karaoke
  P.O. Box 14100
  Nashville, TN 37214-1000
  1-800-795-8925

Telethon

An entire class stages a talent show in the form of a telethon. The event is videotaped for distribution to parents and other classes.

Objectives:

- To allow students to showcase their talents and abilities.

- To promote the performing arts.

Video Equipment and Supplies:

- VCR
- camcorder
- videotapes
- television
- tripod (if available)
- cassette player
- musical instruments
- paper
- pens and pencils
- classroom art supplies
- telephones
- CDs
- markerboard or chalkboard
- pre-recorded segment of Jerry Lewis's Muscular Dystrophy Telethon (if obtainable)

Time: 7–12 hours

Procedure:

1. Play a pre-recorded segment of the Jerry Lewis Muscular Dystrophy Telethon for students or invite those familiar with it to describe it for the class.

2. Discuss the style, format, and purpose of the telethon with students. Explain that they will stage and videotape a make-believe telethon—actually, a talent show. The telethon will not be a true fund-raiser, although it will pretend to be. Emphasize that this is in no way a parody or of the Muscular Dystrophy Telethon—it is a facsimile.

3. Invite students to brainstorm a fictitious cause or organization to sponsor the telethon, such as "Save the Spotted Owl" or "Students United Against Hunger." Designate a research team (3–4 students) to create cue cards containing vital facts about the organization that will be shared with the viewing audience. Encourage creativity and humor here.

4. Distribute a sign-up sheet and invite groups or individuals to sign up for 3-minute performances. Allow space for brief descriptions of the performances on the sheet.

5. Create a schedule based on the completed sign-up sheet. The schedule should include the names of students responsible for operating the camcorder, handling cue cards, or acting as phone operators who accept donations. Announce the date of the telethon.

6. Designate two emcees in whatever way you feel is appropriate. You may wish to have try-outs, ask for volunteers, or have students write letters telling you why they would be a good choice. Emcees will open the show, introduce the talent, ask for contributions, and explain in great detail the urgency of the cause your students have selected. They are responsible for their own scripts. Be sure your emcees understand that they are largely responsible for the pace of the show and may have to ad-lib to conceal minor disasters. Emcees should have a schedule in front of them or on cue cards. Encourage them to dress appropriately.

7. Appoint a team of set designers who will ready the room for the telethon. A tote board for tallying "contributions" is a necessity, as well as a phone bank and performance area.

8. Set a first run-through date at which students will perform their acts for the class to critique. All costumes and props should be ready at this time. Take inventory and offer suggestions at this dress rehearsal. Encourage plenty of rehearsal, both in school and out.

9. Plan on a casual production with lots of ad-libbing. This lends a note of authenticity and adds humor. Emcees will open with dialogue before introducing the first act. Students operating the camcorder should remember to pan to the phone bank occasionally where operators are busily chatting with potential contributors. Another individual can record donations on the tote board. Share the completed video with the class before circulating it to others.

Video Surrealism

Students learn about the surrealist movement, with particular emphasis on the work of painter and sculptor René Magritte. Pairs of students will create representational drawings of new or unexpected "realities." Artwork will be videotaped.

Objectives:

- To acquaint students with Magritte and the surrealist movement in visual arts.
- To encourage the expression of ideas through visual imagery.
- To promote appreciation of the visual arts.

Video Equipment and Supplies:

- VCR
- camcorder
- videotapes
- television
- crayons or pastels
- paper
- pens and pencils
- reference books
- construction paper
- glue sticks
- slides or posters of surrealist art by Magritte

Time:

4–5 hours

Procedure:

1. Share slides or posters of Magritte's work with students. Discuss *surrealism*—an invented word meaning *super-realism*. Consult art history or reference books for information. *Artforms* by D. & S. Preble (Harper & Row) and *Art: Context and Criticism* by J. Kissick (Brown & Benchmark) are both recommended.

2. Briefly discuss the history and significance of *surrealism*—the juxtaposition of recognizable forms in unusual ways to create a feeling of mystery or an alternative reality. Ask for assistance from your fine arts teacher if you are uncomfortable or unfamiliar with the terminology.

3. Explain that some surrealist works reflect the subconscious. Invite students to recall memorable dreams and render a scene from their dreams in pastel or crayon. The scenes must be non-violent and in good taste.

4. Once dream scenes are completed, divide students into pairs. Review the idea of juxtaposing recognizable forms in new ways to create a work of art representing an alternative reality. Encourage students to use scissors, glue, and their imaginations to cut their dream scenes apart and recombine them on construction paper into new artistic statements. The works should have thoughtful titles.

5. Shoot a video that focuses on each piece of artwork for 15 seconds. Share the video with the class, inviting comments as artwork is viewed.

6. Consider extending the activity by inviting students to write poems inspired by their surrealist creations.

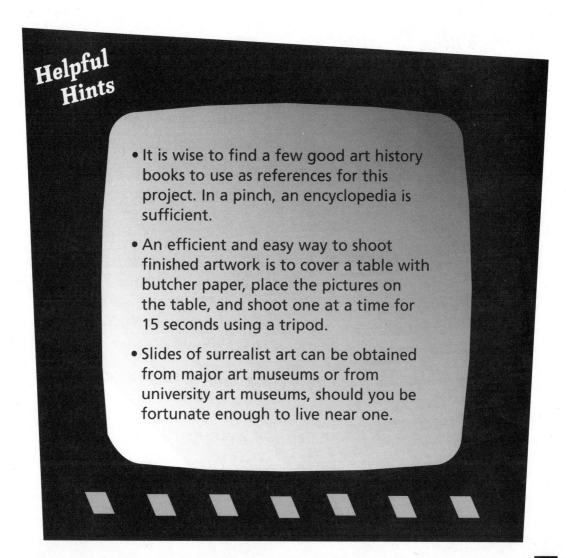

Helpful Hints

- It is wise to find a few good art history books to use as references for this project. In a pinch, an encyclopedia is sufficient.

- An efficient and easy way to shoot finished artwork is to cover a table with butcher paper, place the pictures on the table, and shoot one at a time for 15 seconds using a tripod.

- Slides of surrealist art can be obtained from major art museums or from university art museums, should you be fortunate enough to live near one.

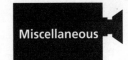

Public Service Announcement

Students create one-minute videos that provide important information concerning the school or community. Videos are circulated via the school library or viewed by large gatherings of students and/or staff.

Objectives:

- To generate student awareness of significant school or community issues.

- To develop a sense of civic responsibility among students.

- To inspire students to devise solutions to social problems.

Video Equipment and Supplies:

- VCR
- camcorder
- videotapes
- television
- pre-recorded public service announcements

- paper
- pens and pencils
- markers
- construction paper
- script and storyboard worksheets on pages 75-76

Time: 3–5 hours

Procedure:

1. Invite students to recall examples of public service ads they have seen on TV, such as "your brain on drugs" or crash-test dummies. Discuss the purpose of such ads with students.

2. Divide students into cooperative groups of 4–6. Have each group choose an issue, problem, or situation to use as the subject of a one-minute public service ad.

3. Encourage groups to develop stories for the ads as well as innovative scripts and/or storyboards. Allocate practice time.

4. You may wish to schedule a dress rehearsal day for students to run their ads for the class to critique.

5. Develop a shooting schedule for the public service ads. Consider enlisting the help of an aide or parent. Make a determination regarding whether or not ads may be shot away from school property using home camcorders.

6. Share completed tapes with students, teachers, or administrators.

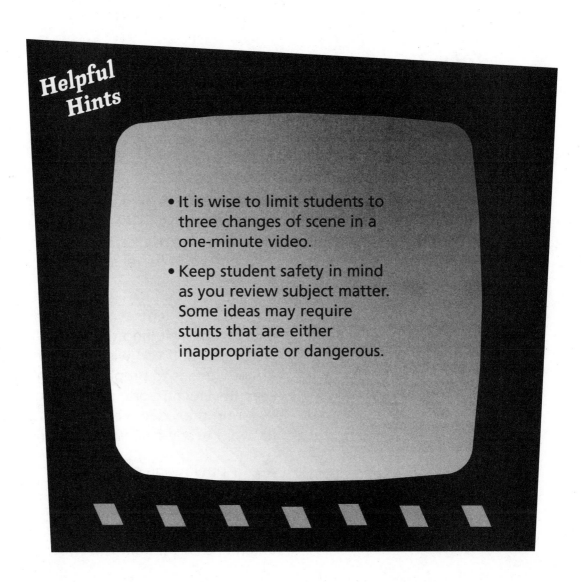

Helpful Hints

- It is wise to limit students to three changes of scene in a one-minute video.

- Keep student safety in mind as you review subject matter. Some ideas may require stunts that are either inappropriate or dangerous.

See You in September

A particular teacher's class or an entire graduating class makes a video of advice and comments for next year's class.

Objectives:

- To offer students the opportunity to reflect upon the past academic year.

- To offer a new class of students insight into the coming year.

- To provide the teacher with constructive comments that can be helpful in planning.

Video Equipment and Supplies:

- VCR
- camcorder
- videotapes
- television
- paper
- pens and pencils

Time: 1–2 hours

Procedure:

1. Invite students to think back on the year and jot down highlights, things they wish they had known in advance, and other observations they feel would be valuable to next year's students.

2. Have students write short, reflective paragraphs including the ideas they have jotted down. If you wish, state that the goal of the video is to prepare students for next year. Review paragraphs with students before shooting the video. Encourage humor and try to avoid overly-zealous censorship.

3. Appoint one or two students to be videographers. Have students read their paragraphs once off-camera and once for the camcorder. Save the tape to use at the beginning of the following year.

The Year in Review

Students keep a concise video record of the events of the school year–a form of video yearbook.

Objectives:

- To encourage student awareness of important lessons, projects, and events.

- To instill lasting memories of the school year.

- To prod students to contemplate pivotal moments of their school year.

Video Equipment and Supplies:

- VCR
- camcorder
- videotapes
- television
- paper
- pens and pencils
- classroom art supplies
- construction paper

Time: Varies

Procedure:

1. At the beginning of the year, explain to students that they will be keeping a video log of important events throughout the year. The video will feature items of interest both in and out of the classroom.

2. Specify a tape approximately 90 minutes in length with segments of approximately 15 seconds each. This ends up being a total of 360 segments—about 40 per month.

3. At the beginning of each week or month, create a schedule of events to be covered. Assign crews of students to tape each one. Keep in mind that events may come up which have not been scheduled but which should be included on the video. Keep track of what has been shot and for how long to have an accurate read on how much tape time is left.

4. Invite a volunteer to create a title to shoot at the beginning of the tape that includes the name of the school and the year.

5. Help students understand the importance of being discerning as they fill their 15 seconds. Students should choose important moments, such as the crowning of the Valentine King and Queen or the opening tip-off of the championship game, rather than random scenes of a school dance or sports event.

6. Share the completed video with the class, or several classes, at the end of the year. Students may wish to add a closing commentary on any blank tape remaining.

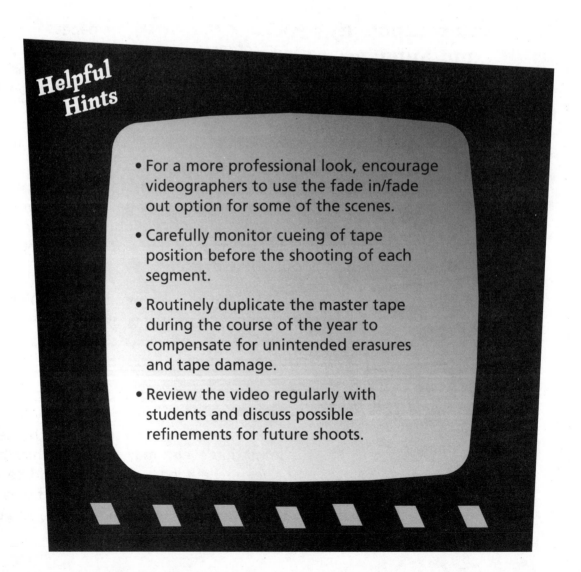

Helpful Hints

- For a more professional look, encourage videographers to use the fade in/fade out option for some of the scenes.

- Carefully monitor cueing of tape position before the shooting of each segment.

- Routinely duplicate the master tape during the course of the year to compensate for unintended erasures and tape damage.

- Review the video regularly with students and discuss possible refinements for future shoots.

Video Portfolio

Cooperative groups or individuals shoot video portfolios of selected "benchmark" activities or assignments that demonstrate what students have learned from a particular unit or lesson.

Objectives:

- To allow teachers to assess student learning.
- To include students in the evaluation process.
- To increase student interest in a thematic unit by allowing them to concentrate on areas of interest.

Video Equipment and Supplies:

- VCR
- camcorder
- videotapes
- tripod
- classroom supplies as needed for individual lessons
- script and/or storyboard worksheets on pages 75–76
- television
- paper
- pens and pencils

Time: Varies

Procedure:

1. At the outset of the thematic unit, explain to students that they will be responsible for shooting 3–5 minute videos that include five examples of assignments and/or activities from the unit. Selected examples should exhibit the highest quality of work and level of learning achieved by each student. Students are responsible for choosing the items on their videos. An example from a social studies unit on Ancient Greece is provided on page 71.

2. Set a due date for the completed videos.

3. Have students complete scripts and/or storyboards for your approval before shooting their videos. Encourage unique and innovative approaches.

4. Create a schedule for use of the school camcorder if necessary. Encourage students to use home camcorders where available.

5. Share completed videos with the class over a period of several days.

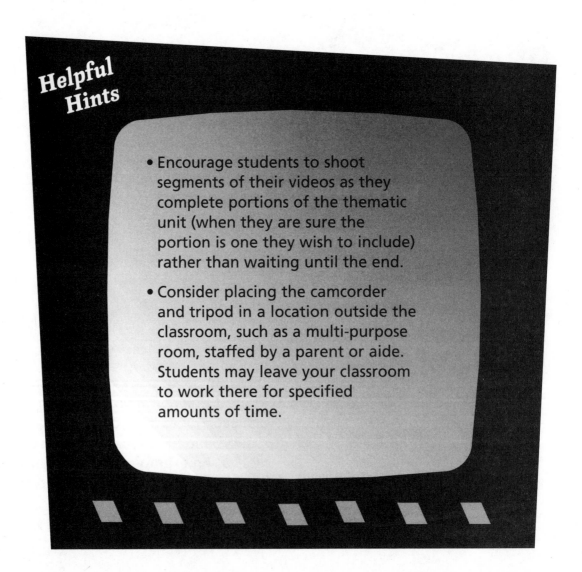

Helpful Hints

- Encourage students to shoot segments of their videos as they complete portions of the thematic unit (when they are sure the portion is one they wish to include) rather than waiting until the end.

- Consider placing the camcorder and tripod in a location outside the classroom, such as a multi-purpose room, staffed by a parent or aide. Students may leave your classroom to work there for specified amounts of time.

Sample Script: Video Portfolio

Scene	Audio	Video
1	**Introduction** The map you see shows the country of Greece. It is a peninsula located in the Mediterranean Sea. To the east of Greece is the Aegean Sea. To the west is the Ionian Sea. The map shows some important locations of Ancient Greece. *Student continues to discuss various key points on map, such as Athens, Olympia, and Delphi.*	Close-up of student-drawn map of Ancient Greece.
2	Somewhere between 3000 and 1000 B.C., people began to settle in Greece. One of the earliest known settlements is the forts at Mycenae. Around 1200 B.C., Greece was at war with neighboring Troy. The war was called the Trojan War . . . . *Student continues to discuss key points on time line.*	Close-up of student-drawn time line of Ancient Greece.
3	Mythology was very important to the ancient Greeks. The Greeks believed in many gods and goddesses whom they thought ruled all aspects of life. Many stories, or myths, were created about these gods and goddesses and their dealings with the Greek people. One of my favorite myths is the myth of Daedalus and Icarus. As you recall from our history book, Daedalus and Icarus made wings from feathers and wax in order to fly away from the island of Crete, where they were held captive by King Minos. I have written a sequel to the myth. *Student reads original myth sequel.*	Medium shot of student speaking into camcorder microphone. Close-up of student drawings that correspond to myth.

Sample Script: Video Portfolio

Scene	Audio	Video
4	The ancient Greeks are also famous for their architecture. One of the most famous works of Greek architecture is the Parthenon.	Medium shot of student standing next to model of Parthenon.
	The ancient Greeks began building the Parthenon around 447 B.C. When it was completed, the Parthenon was more than 200 feet long, about 100 feet wide, and about 65 feet high. It was created as a shrine to the goddess Athena. I have built a model of the Parthenon. Notice the rows of Doric columns that surround the Parthenon	Close-up of student model of Parthenon.
5	The Greek alphabet differs from our alphabet. It consists of 24 letters: alpha, beta, gamma, delta	Close-up of student-made chart of Greek alphabet. Student points to letters as she reads them.
	Here are some examples of Greek words. *Student gives Greek pronunciation followed by English translation of several words.*	Close-up of student-made scroll. Selected Greek words are inscribed on the scroll, which is unrolled to bring words into view as they are read.

Welcome to Our School

Students create and shoot a video designed to provide new students with information that will facilitate their transition to a new school.

Objectives:

- To instill in students a sense of pride in their school.

- To focus students' attention on positive features of their school.

- To help new students feel welcome and to familiarize them with the school.

- To teach empathy for students in new and strange situations.

Video Equipment and Supplies:

- VCR
- camcorder
- videotapes
- television
- script and/or storyboard worksheets on pages 75–76
- paper
- pens and pencils
- markers
- classroom art supplies

Time: 5–8 hours

Procedure:

1. Explain to students that they will be shooting a 10–12 minute video designed to help new students feel comfortable in their school.

2. Encourage students to imagine they are new in school. Brainstorm with students a list of facts they feel would be valuable to new students. List them on the board.

3. Have students vote to determine ten items to be included on their video. Decide on the order of the ten segments. Set a date for completion.

4. Divide students into cooperative groups of 4–6. Each group will produce a segment of the video that addresses 2–3 of the ten chosen items. In addition, one group will take responsibility for an introduction and one for the conclusion.

5. Invite groups to create scripts or storyboards detailing their ideas for your approval. Scripts should include segues to the next group's segment. Circulate among groups as they work to offer assistance and facilitate continuity of vision.

6. Encourage groups to create cue cards for their portion of the video. Insist on adequate rehearsal by each group. Create a shooting schedule that allows time for three takes per group.

7. Check that groups have cued the tape properly before they begin shooting. Each group should begin its segment with a 5-second establishing shot and end with 5 seconds of non-audio footage to prevent unintentional erasures of dialogue.

8. Share the completed video with the class. Make copies to distribute to new families in the community.

Helpful Hints

- You may wish to establish a particular format for all groups, such as documentary or infomercial. This will add consistency to the overall look of the video.

- Since students will be shooting their segments consecutively, proper cueing of the tape is critical.

- Remind students to obtain permission from other staff members, when required, for their segments.

- Consider having a parent or aide accompany groups as they shoot their segments.

Script

page_____

Scene	Audio	Video

Storyboard

Scene	Description	Picture	Time

Running Time_____

Pre-Taping Checklist

This checklist will help ensure the success of your video production. Check each item just before you begin to shoot your video to verify that your preparations are complete.

_____ 1. Conditions at taping location are favorable.

> *Consider crowds, weather, background noise, equipment security, ease of access, possible disruptions and distractions, optimum time to tape, safety.*

_____ 2. Permission to tape has been obtained.

_____ 3. Crew is informed of time, location, and duration of taping.

_____ 4. Camera angles have been selected.

_____ 5. Crew has necessary equipment in its possession.

> *Consider camcorder, VCR, fully-charged batteries, cables, notepads, pens, tripod, videotape.*

_____ 6. Props, scenery, and costumes are available if needed.

_____ 7. Sufficient tape stock exists.

_____ 8. On-screen and off-screen job assignments are understood.

_____ 9. Cueing methods are understood. Cue cards are present if required.

> *Consider method of cueing both videographer and talent.*

_____ 10. Sufficient electrical outlets are available.

_____ 11. Lighting is adequate.

> *Consider position and intensity of sun, adequacy of indoor light source, additional lighting if necessary.*

_____ 12. Tape is cued to proper position.

_____ 13. Segment has been properly rehearsed.

_____ 14. Shooting sequence has been planned and is understood by crew.

On-Line Computer Networks

On-line computer networks, such as the Internet and CompuServe, provide excellent meeting places for teachers and students to exchange videos for Distance Debate or to share original projects.

Following is a list of some forums you may wish to investigate.

The Internet

Kidlink Project: a network providing global dialogue for students age 10–15 through e-mail and telecommunications. Kidlink can be accessed at gopher://kids.duq.edu

Global School House: a nationwide project designed to connect schools on the Internet. Global School House can be accessed at janice@cnidr.org *or* gfitz@cerf.net

Worldwide Education Network: a worldwide forum through which educators can specify their educational interests and contact educators with similar interests. Worldwide Education Network can be accessed at worldwide@csupomona.edu

CompuServe

CompuServe Education Forum: a national forum through which educators can communicate ideas and projects. CompuServe Education Forum can be accessed at GO:EDFORUM

Students Forum: a national forum through which students and teachers can communicate ideas and projects. Student Forum can be accessed at GO:STUFO

Consult the Internet Yellow Pages or the CompuServe Yellow Pages at your community library or bookstore for an in-depth listing of educational forums and bulletin boards.

A word of caution: should you contact teachers outside of North America, chances are your videotapes will not play in their VCRs, and vice versa. Televisions and VCRs in North America generally adhere to NTSC (National Television System Committee) standards. Be sure your partner in any exchange video project shares this system.

Glossary

Audio signal: the sound recorded or transmitted by a camcorder or VCR.

Backdrop: decoration at the rear of a stage.

Background music: low-level music recorded on a videotape.

Camera angle: position of camcorder in relation to subject.

Close-up: shot emphasizing a person's face or specific detail in a scene.

Cue: to prompt video crew members to begin action; to position videotape in a specific location.

Cue card: card held out of camcorder view containing dialogue to be read by person(s) being videotaped.

Cue tape: positioning videotape in the proper location required for a particular scene by moving it forward or backward (*rewind* or *fast forward*).

Cut: transition to another shot.

Dollying: moving the camcorder toward or away from the subject during shooting. It captures movement in a more natural way than zooming and usually involves rolling the camcorder on a wheeled support stand.

Edit: to arrange sequence of shots recorded on videotape or remove unwanted material.

Establishing shot: a shot that opens a scene by showing entire area in which action will occur.

Extreme close-up: a shot that emphasizes minute detail.

Fade in: solid color, usually black or white, diminishing to a distinct picture.

Fade out: picture gradually diminishing to solid color, usually black or white.

Footage: amount (length) of videotape consumed by a particular scene or series of scenes.

Gaffer: person handling physical duties associated with production, such as moving equipment and winding cable.

Input selection button: button that tells VCR which jack the video signal is coming through.

Karaoke™ tape: recording of the instrumental portion of a popular song.

Mark: particular spot on which individuals are positioned or stand during shooting.

Medium shot: shot mid-way between close-up and wide shot that includes a few details and significant background.

Miscue: tape not cued to proper position or action prompted at the wrong time.

Moderate angle shot: camcorder positioned to give slight side view of subject being videotaped.

Montage: many shots combined to make a scene or entire video.

Off-camera: individuals or objects not being recorded by camcorder.

On-camera: individuals or objects being recorded by camcorder.

Pan: moving camcorder horizontally from a stationary position to cover action in a scene.

Panoramic shot: shot providing unobstructed view of vast area.

Post-production: changes made to videotape with editing equipment after shooting is completed.

Production value: aspects of a videotape that make it appear smoother or more professional.

Real time: the time during which the camcorder is recording, as opposed to post-production.

Scene: single episode or portion of a video; segment.

Script: written text of a video.

Segment: single episode or portion of a video; scene.

Shot: portion of video recorded by one camcorder without interruption.

Sound effects: incidental sounds added to create or enhance a mood or effect.

Storyboard: sequence of drawings and explanations outlining a video concept.

Take: one recording of a single shot.

Talent: broad term used to denote anyone appearing on-screen in a designated role.

Tilt: moving camcorder vertically to capture a subject.

Transition: change from one scene or shot to next scene or shot.

Tripod: three-legged stand that supports a camcorder.

TV/Video button: button on VCR that designates whether it will play videotapes or TV channels.

Video-in jack: connecting device on VCR or camcorder through which it receives an external video signal via cable for processing.

Videographer: person operating the camcorder.

Video-out jack: connecting device on VCR or camcorder through which it transmits an external signal via cable for processing.

Video signal: visual images recorded or transmitted by camcorder or VCR.

Viewfinder: eyepiece on a camcorder through which videographer views subject being recorded.

Wide shot: shot providing an unobstructed view of a vast area.

Zoom: to make an image appear larger or smaller by focusing the camera lens.